Contents

Any words appearing in the text in bold, **like this**,
are explained in the Glossary.

What is an allergy?

An allergy happens when a person's body reacts badly to something that is usually harmless to other people. If someone in your school has allergies, it simply means that if they come into contact with certain things, like house dust or animal fur, they may become unwell. This is called an allergic reaction. For many people these **symptoms** may be irritating, but fairly mild. They may get a runny nose, sore eyes or a rash on their skin. For others the allergic reaction can be sudden and quite severe. If it is, they may need medicine to soothe the symptoms. In just a few extreme cases, allergies can kill.

Most allergic reactions are not too serious. People may just get a runny nose and sore eyes. Even so, it can be hard to concentrate on schoolwork if you feel poorly like this every day.

Allergens

The substance (or stuff) that causes an allergic reaction is called an **allergen**. Allergens get into the body in one of four ways.

- Some allergens are breathed in with air, such as **pollen**, dust or **dander** (animal fur and/or skin).
- Some are injected, such as insect stings or a few medicines.
- Some are swallowed, such as food allergens.
- Some people have allergic reactions if they touch certain things, such as some plants.

What does it mean to have

Allergies

Louise Spilsbury

Heinemann
LIBRARY

www.heinemann.co.uk/library
Visit our website to find out more information about Heinemann Library books.

To order:
☎ Phone 44 (0) 1865 888066
▤ Send a fax to 44 (0) 1865 314091
▣ Visit the Heinemann Bookshop at www.heinemann.co.uk/library to browse our catalogue and order online.

First published in Great Britain by Heinemann Library,
Halley Court, Jordan Hill, Oxford OX2 8EJ,
a division of Reed Educational and Professional Publishing Ltd.
Heinemann is a registered trademark of Reed Educational and Professional Publishing Ltd.

OXFORD MELBOURNE AUCKLAND
JOHANNESBURG BLANTYRE GABORONE
IBADAN PORTSMOUTH (NH) USA CHICAGO

Designed by AMR
Originated by Dot Gradations
Printed in China by WKT

ISBN 978 0 431 13921 0 (hardback)
06 05 04 03 02
10 9 8 7 6 5 4 3 2

ISBN 978 0 431 13928 9
07
10 9 8 7 6 5 4 3 2

British Library Cataloguing in Publication Data
Spilsbury, Louise
  What does it mean to have allergies?
  1.Allergy
  I.Title II.Allergies
  616.9'7

FIFE COUNCIL WEST AREA	
791088	
PETERS	21-Aug-07
J616.97	£6.99
JME	DP

Acknowledgements
The publishers would like to thank the following for permission to reproduce photographs:
Bubbles/Pauline Cutler, p.4; Bruce Coleman Collection/Jane Burton, p.22, /Kim Taylow, p.27; Oxford Scientific Films/Martyn Chillmaid, p.25; Pictor International, pp.23, 24; Powerstock Zefa/Benelux Press, p.26; Science Photo Library, p.19, /Mark Clarke, p.7, /BSIP Edwige, p.9, /Dr Kari Lounatmaa, p.6, /Andrew Syred, p.14; Tony Stone Images/Lori Adamski Peek, pp.8, 21, /Pam Francis, p.29; Telegraph Colour Library/Jade Albert Studios, Inc, p.11, /Paul King, p.5, /Planet Earth/Mark Mattock, p.18;
All other photography taken on commission by Trevor Clifford.

The pictures on the following pages were posed by models who do not have allergies: 5, 8, 10–13, 16–17, 20–21, 23–25, 29.

Special thanks to: Chantal, Charlotte, Christopher, Emma, George, James, Jonathan, Josi, Kirsty and Lauren.

The publishers would like to thank: Action Against Allergies, and Dr Richard Turner, Allergy Specialist, Northampton Hospital, Basingstoke, for their advice and support. Also Julie Johnson, PHSE Consultant Trainer and Writer, for her help in the preparation of this book.

What causes allergies?

In this book you can find out about some of the substances that many young people are allergic to – certain kinds of food, house-dust mites, pollen and insect stings. However, people can be allergic to anything – from milkshakes to toilet rolls – and the same allergen can set off different reactions in different people.

Curiously, the thing that sets off allergic reactions is the very thing that is meant to protect people from harm. The **immune system** is the body's defence system and it is vital for keeping us well. It's just that in people who have allergies, their immune system reacts to things that are not usually harmful – and those reactions can be unpleasant. Nevertheless, most allergies can be controlled or treated, leaving people to get on with leading full and happy lives.

Allergy facts

- The number of people who have allergies is increasing.
- One in three people will have an allergy at some time in their life.
- Around one in ten people will have a food allergy at some time in their life.

Most people find ways of controlling their allergies, so they can get on with doing the things they enjoy.

What is your immune system?

Your **immune system** does a very important job: it defends your body against disease. It seeks out any unwanted substances that get into your body – such as **germs** – and destroys them. Your blood plays a major part in your immune system. When germs get into your body, it recognizes quickly that chemicals on the germs, called **antigens**, are not part of your body. First, special **white blood cells** go to work. They make chemicals called **antibodies** that attach themselves to the germs. Once the germs are covered with antibodies, other white blood cells can find them and move in for the kill.

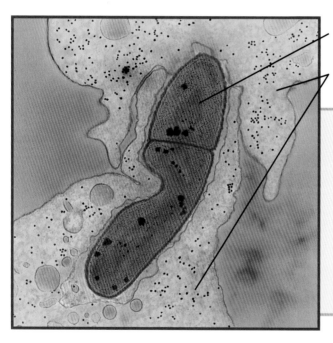

bacteria

white blood cells

White blood cells help you to fight illnesses by destroying germs. This picture shows two white blood cells at work, attacking germs called bacteria. (The white cells have been coloured blue, to make it easier to see them.)

Vaccines

You have probably had several vaccinations in your life. Vaccines are made from dead germs. Doctors or nurses put a tiny amount of the germ that causes a particular disease into your body. This vaccine encourages your body to make antibodies against the disease. This means your body is ready to destroy that disease if you should ever come into contact with the live germs.

Allergic reactions

Normally, our immune system protects us from substances that could harm us. People who have allergies have an immune system that not only reacts to germs, but also reacts to substances that are usually harmless to most other people. This is because their immune system is too good at its job. It makes too much of a special antibody called Immunoglobulin E, or IgE for short.

When a person has an allergy, their immune system produces lots of these IgE antibodies. When the body takes in a substance to which it is allergic – an **allergen** – these special IgE antibodies attack it. In the ensuing battle, chemicals, such as **histamine**, are released. It is these chemicals that cause the **symptoms** of an allergic reaction, such as swollen, itchy, red skin, watery eyes, sneezing, even sickness and diarrhoea. For example, when histamine is released into your nose, it makes you sneeze and makes your nose run. If histamine is released into your **lungs**, it makes you wheeze.

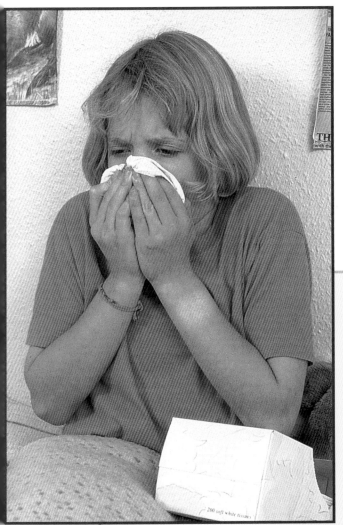

This is what can happen when someone with an allergy comes into contact with an allergen (substance that sets off an allergic reaction). The special allergy antibodies in their immune system cause the release of chemicals that make them feel unwell.

Who gets allergies?

Some people have certain similarities to their parents, like the colour of their eyes or the shape of their nose. This is because people **inherit** particular characteristics from their parents. Allergies tend to run in families like this. If their mother

or father, or another close family member, has allergies, there is a chance that their child might have allergies, too. If both parents have allergies, their children have about a 75 per cent chance of becoming allergic. If only one parent is allergic, or if relatives on only one side of the family have allergies, the child has about a 50 per cent (one in two) chance of developing allergies.

Even if children inherit a tendency to being allergic from their parents, they may not develop allergies. And if they do, they may not be allergic to the same things as their parents!

Are brothers and sisters useful?

You may find this hard to believe, but brothers and sisters can be useful! Many doctors think that young children who catch infections from older brothers and sisters have less chance of getting allergies. While your body is busy making lots of **antibodies** to destroy the infections, it cannot make allergy antibodies at the same time.

Allergy puzzles

Finding out whether someone has an allergy, and exactly what form that allergy takes, is a tricky business. It's like putting together a difficult jigsaw puzzle. Doctors gradually have to build up a complete picture of that person and their health. They have to ask a lot of questions to find out more about the possible allergic reactions they or their families have had in the past. They also do a physical examination of the person to check that their body is well. Finally, doctors look at the results of any allergy tests that have been done.

Skin prick tests

The **skin prick test** is one of the most useful tests for finding what causes someone's allergic reaction. Tiny amounts of the suspected **allergens**, such as **pollen** or **dander**, are put into the skin on the front of the arm with a small, thin **lancet**. If the person develops an itchy red bump bigger than 3mm, it means they are allergic to that particular substance. The bigger the bump, the more sensitive the person is to that allergen. The lump goes down quite quickly and the test is perfectly safe.

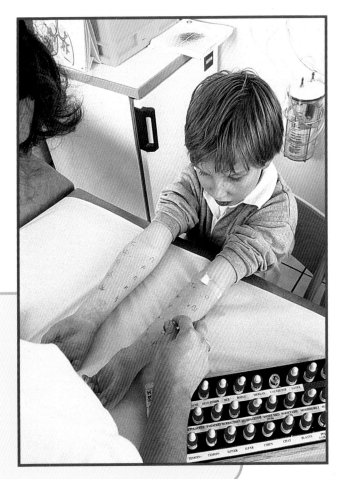

This boy is having a skin prick test to find out what he is allergic to. The lancet is very small and it feels a bit uncomfortable, but it does not really hurt.

Allergies from food

Most of us choose what to eat because we like the way a particular food tastes or we like the look of it. People with allergies to certain foods have to be more careful about what they eat.

Food allergies cause many different **symptoms** including itching or swelling of the lips and tongue, a tight or sensitive throat, a rash, wheezing, itchy eyes and a stomach upset. For some people, symptoms start as soon as the food touches their lips. For others it may take several hours before allergic reactions occur.

Problem foods?

A person can be allergic to any kind of food, but these are the foods that most often set off allergies.

- Cow's milk.
- Eggs.
- Wheat.
- Peanuts.
- Soya beans – lots of products are made from soya beans, including tofu and soya sauce, and many other foods and ready-made meals contain a small amount of them.
- Nuts from trees, such as almonds or brazil nuts.
- Fish.
- Shellfish, such as prawns, mussels, crab or lobster.

Many people with food allergies have to check the ingredients of ready-made foods before they eat them. This is because they may contain tiny amounts of the food to which they are allergic.

Eczema

Around one in twenty people get an allergic reaction called **eczema**. Different people have different kinds of eczema, but most eczema causes itching and a red rash. In some cases it can cause blisters and feel hot, too. If you scratch eczema too much it can get infected and you may need to take medicines called **antibiotics** to clear it up. Some people who have eczema get fed up with it not only because it is sore, but also because of the way it looks, especially if they get it somewhere that shows, such as on the hands or face.

Eczema can be caused by an allergic reaction to certain foods, such as milk. It may also be caused by **allergens** that surround us, which we either touch or breathe in, like dust or **pollen**. Some people find they get eczema when they are feeling low or are upset about something. If eczema is caused by a food, then people can try to avoid eating that food. Doctors can also give people creams that help to get rid of the rash.

*Eczema looks sore, but it is not **contagious**. You cannot catch it from holding hands with or touching someone who has it.*

Treating food allergies

Before a person can deal with a food allergy, they need to know which food they are allergic to. Some people do a bit of detective work of their own. They keep a diary of the foods they eat and when they feel ill. After two weeks, they may notice that an allergic reaction comes after eating a particular food.

Doctors might suggest they stop eating the foods they suspect may cause the reactions for a short time. For example, they might try avoiding milk for a week or two. If the **symptoms** don't stop, they leave out another food. This can be done with different foods, one at a time, until they find the culprit.

Once people know which food causes their allergy, they can avoid eating it. That is not quite as easy as it sounds. There are lots of hidden ingredients in foods we buy, and lots of things we may not know about, like eggs or milk in mayonnaise, or nuts in chocolate bars. Once a person stops eating the food, the reactions to it usually stop very quickly. Sometimes more severe (stronger) reactions may take longer to disappear.

When people with food allergies go out for a meal, they often check the ingredients of the food they want before they order.

Meet Molly

I'm Molly and I'm eleven years old now. I found out that I had an allergy to peanuts when I was six. I guess I didn't really try peanuts until then. Apart from the peanut allergy I'm really healthy. I'm a vegetarian and I'm careful about what I eat anyway.

Lots of people have peanut allergies. I have heard of people who have to be really careful. If they eat just one peanut, they could die. I have never had a serious reaction, but I still always avoid eating peanuts.

My allergy can be a real chore sometimes. All sorts of foods have tiny bits of nut in, like chocolate bars, ready-made meals, cakes, pastries and pies. My mum and I spend ages reading labels in the supermarket. These days most companies put stickers on their foods, telling you if there are any nuts in them, but it's still best to check everything.

All my friends know about my peanut allergy. It's better if you tell people. My friends know that it's really important for me to avoid peanuts and that I'm not just being fussy.

Hidden nuisance: house-dust mites

In the dust that builds up in the nooks and crannies of all our homes is a hidden nuisance – the house-dust mite. These tiny mites are only 0.3 mm long, which is even smaller than the head of a pin. They are also transparent (see-through) so they are almost invisible to the human eye. House-dust mites eat tiny bits of skin that we have shed. They thrive in bedding, carpeting, sofas and chairs. Most of us never even know they are there and they don't cause most of us any trouble at all.

However, some people get an allergic reaction to the house-dust mite's droppings. These droppings are so tiny and light that when you flop down on a sofa or run across a carpet they are shaken up into the air. Many stay in the air, floating about and people breathe them in with the air. When some people breathe them in, they get an allergic reaction.

When you look at an enlarged photo of a house-dust mite, like this one, it looks like some kind of ugly monster. Don't worry – in reality they are so small you could not see one without the help of a microscope. This one was magnified (made bigger) by about 200 times so it could be photographed.

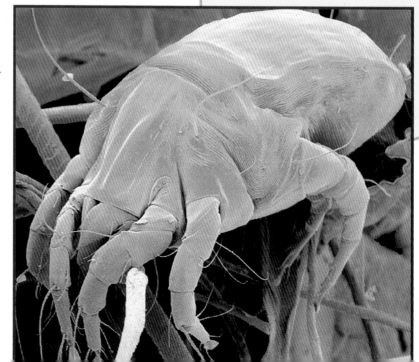

What happens?

House-dust mite droppings cause different reactions in different people. Some people sneeze and have a runny nose. Doctors call this **rhinitis**. If it lasts only for a month or two it is called seasonal rhinitis. Sometimes the **symptoms** last for longer, for example some people have a runny nose all the time, which gets blocked as well. This is called perennial rhinitis. Rhinitis can make people feel miserable and it makes it hard to concentrate on schoolwork or anything else. House-dust mites are also a major **trigger** for people with allergic **eczema** and **asthma**.

Asthma

People with asthma have sensitive airways (the breathing tubes that take air from your nose or mouth to your **lungs** so you can breathe). This means the tubes are often sore and swollen. They are quick to react to anything that irritates them, including house-dust mite droppings. The airways swell up so the space for air to get through becomes narrower. It becomes harder for the person to breathe. They may also start coughing, have a tight feeling in their chest or wheeze. Most children control their asthma by taking medicines.

*House-dust mite's droppings are an airborne **allergen**. That means that people take them in through their nose or mouth with the air that they breathe.*

Taking action

People who are allergic to house-dust mites use two means of attack on their tiny enemies. They take medicines to stop the **symptoms** caused by the allergic reaction and they take steps to avoid coming into contact with the droppings. It is virtually impossible to rid your home of every bit of dust but there are lots of things people with allergies can do to limit the dust and make their home a less appealing place for mites to live in.

People with dust mite allergies should always put their clothes away. Piles of clothes all over the floor make an ideal home for house-dust mites!

Give dust mites their marching orders!

Here are just a few of the tactics people use to make their bedroom a dust-free zone.

- Use special covers on the mattress, pillows and duvet to stop dust getting into them.
- House-dust mites love warm, stuffy rooms, so open the windows often.
- Dust surfaces with a damp cloth so you don't just brush the dust into the air.
- Vacuum often, using a cleaner with a good, strong sucking power.
- Choose wooden flooring, tiles or lino instead of carpets, and use rugs, which can be washed often.
- Wash bedding at high temperatures or put cuddly toys in the freezer overnight to kill the mites off.

Meet Miles

My name is Miles and I'm ten years old. I have been allergic to house-dust mites for as long as I can remember. House dust brings on my **asthma** and then I start coughing a lot. I use an **inhaler** every day to help, and when I have an asthma attack I have to take another kind of medicine to help me stop coughing. Using the inhaler is a bit of a drag sometimes, but at least it makes me feel better.

At home I've got things pretty much under control. There are wooden floor boards in the living room, and my bedroom is a real dust-free zone. Here too, I've got wooden floors and

special covers on my bed and pillows to stop any dust getting out of the mattress into the air. It's when I want to stay over at a friend's house the problems can start. So mostly they come here. I've got bunk beds so they can stay in my room and then it's OK. I always sleep on the top bunk as it's less dusty on top.

Hay fever

Hay fever is a common allergic reaction caused by **pollen**. Pollen is the name for the tiny grains released by trees, grasses, weeds and flowers in the spring and summer months. Pollen is released from the flower of one plant so that it can land in the flower of another plant of the same kind, where it helps to make seeds. These seeds can grow into new plants after they are released.

Pollen grains are so tiny we cannot see them, but on some spring or summer days they can fill the air. When pollen blows into the eyes, nose or throat of people who get hay fever, it sets off an allergic reaction.

Pollen is small and light enough to be carried long distances on the wind. This means it is a problem for people in towns and cities as well as in the country.

Facts about hay fever

- There are lots of different kinds of pollen. Some people are only allergic to one or two, others are allergic to lots of different kinds.
- Grass pollen causes most people's hay fever.
- Tree pollen also causes hay fever.

What are the symptoms?

Most people who suffer from hay fever find that as soon as they breathe in pollen grains, their body reacts. The pollen **allergens** irritate the delicate linings of the nose, throat, eyes and **lungs**. Different people get different **symptoms**, and while some people may only get one symptom, others may get several at once. Symptoms include:

- sneezing
- wheezing
- itchy, blocked or runny nose
- red, itchy or watery eyes
- itchy throat, ears or mouth
- headaches
- generally feeling unwell.

When a person's body reacts to pollen, their **immune system** wages war on the tiny grains. As part of its attack, the immune system makes **histamine** and other irritating chemicals. These substances are what cause the bad reactions. People use medicines called **antihistamines** to soothe the reactions. They work by stopping many of the effects of histamine. People can take antihistamines in tablets, syrup, eye drops or sprays.

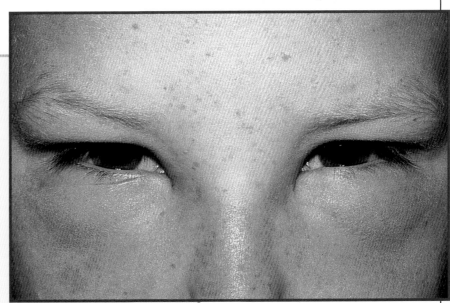

For thousands of young people who get hay fever, sore, itchy eyes and a runny nose can make it very hard to get down to schoolwork.

Controlling hay fever

As well as using medicines to soothe their **symptoms**, many people control their hay fever by avoiding **pollen**. One of the easiest ways of avoiding pollen is to stay indoors when there is a lot of it about. People know when there is a lot of pollen in the air because they check the pollen count. The pollen count is a measure of how much pollen there is in their area. In summer, weather forecasts usually include a pollen count so that hay fever sufferers can choose to stay indoors when it is high.

Hay fever sufferers check the pollen forecast in newspaper reports or on the TV or radio to find out how high or low the pollen count is in their area.

Things to do

Here are a few of the things hay fever sufferers can do to cut down on the amount of pollen they come into contact with.

- Keep windows closed at home when the pollen count is high, so pollen does not get into the house.
- Dry sheets and pillow cases inside when the pollen count is high.
- Wear sunglasses to stop pollen blowing into their eyes.
- Stay away from places with lots of grass, such as fields.
- Keep out of the way when the grass is mowed, because this can create clouds of pollen.

Meet Joseph

I first got hay fever four years ago when I was nearly six. Ever since then I get it every summer. I get an itchy nose and watery eyes and I sneeze a lot. I get tired too, because I can't sleep properly. I have to take medicines called **antihistamines** as soon as the symptoms start. If the itchy nose still doesn't stop and gets really sore I have another special medicine, which I can spray in my nose.

Sometimes in summer it's quite bad. My eyes start watering and my nose starts itching as soon as I go outside. Then I have to stay indoors and read my books and listen to my music while everyone else is playing in the garden. I'm OK at school because I always remember to take my medicine with me. Then I can play outside at break and do games outside like everyone else. Last year we went to the seaside for our summer holidays and it was really good. My mum said there was less pollen around because of the fresh air blowing in from the sea.

Allergies from pets

Around seven out of ten homes have a pet, usually a cat or a dog. Pets can be a lot of fun. They keep you company or play with you and looking after them can be a great way to learn what animals need to live. However, lots of people are allergic to the animals many of us keep as pets.

When old bits of skin and hair fall off animals such as cats and dogs, it collects around the house. The **allergens** on these substances are very tiny and they float in the air. If they get into someone's eyes or nose, they can make them red, sore and itchy. If they are breathed in, they can make people cough and wheeze and make it hard for them to breathe easily.

The trouble with being clean

Cats are usually clean animals. They spend much of their time grooming – licking themselves to clean their fur. Unfortunately, this causes problems for people with pet allergies. When the saliva (spit) on their fur dries, it becomes airborne. That means it floats in the air. When people with pet allergies breathe it in, it can set off their **symptoms**.

*Some people mistakenly think that their allergy is caused by long-haired animals only. It's the **dander** that causes most allergies, not the amount or length of hair on the pet.*

Finding out

The trouble with pet allergies is that people often refuse to believe that their pet could be the problem. They may think their allergic reaction is caused by something else, like house dust or **pollen**. One way of checking what causes an allergy is a **skin prick test**. In this, tiny amounts of different allergens are scratched into a person's skin. If they get a red bump in that area, it means they are probably allergic to that allergen.

The other way of checking if someone has a pet allergy is for him or her to stay somewhere else where there are no pets for a while. It is not good enough to take the pet away. Even after a really good clean-up, allergens can still hang about in the air for a long time. If the person stays away for a few weeks and their symptoms disappear, it is highly likely that they have a pet allergy.

Treating pet allergies

For many people, the only real solution to a pet allergy is to find a new home for the pet. Yet lots of people love their pets and do not want to do this. If you have a pet, imagine how you would feel if someone suddenly told you it had to go.

If a person cannot bear the thought of giving up their pet, they can try to lessen the problem by doing other things. They can keep the pet outdoors as much as possible, and never let it in the bedrooms. They can wash any bedding or cushions the animal sleeps on, and also the animal itself, if possible.

If someone's allergy is really bad, they may have no choice but to give away the animal. They may be able to get another kind of pet. Most people who have a pet allergy are allergic to animals with fur or feathers. The best kinds of pets for people with allergies are often fish, snakes, lizards, turtles and tortoises. People may also need to take medicines called **antihistamines** to soothe their **symptoms** if they do come into contact with a pet at school or while they are at someone else's house.

Birds can cause allergies, too. Some people are allergic to their droppings and feathers.

Meet Josie

My name is Josie. I am allergic to lots of animals like rabbits and budgies, or horses, cats and dogs. As soon as I get close to one I start coughing and sneezing and I feel really awful. Sometimes the only way to stop it is to take some of my medicine.

It can be a problem sometimes. When I was younger they had to get rid of the class rabbit because it made me ill when I was at school. I also have to be really careful when I visit friends' houses. It is OK at my best friend's because she knows to keep her cat out of her room. I sometimes take an antihistamine before I go, and that stops the symptoms.

I have got a pet – a snake. At first some of my friends thought it was a really strange idea. Then my teacher asked me to bring it into class and give a talk about it. I took in an old skin that she had shed as well. Silky is a really lovely snake and everyone thought she was brilliant. I think she is much more interesting than most other pets!

Insect alert!

Most of us are a little scared of being stung by insects like wasps and bees. Stings can be itchy and sore. For most of us, these **symptoms** usually go away by themselves within a couple of hours or days. For some people, however, insect stings can **trigger** an allergic reaction, which can be much nastier.

Allergic reactions are different for different people. Some people get very bad itching and a large swelling around the area of the sting, and even in other parts of their body, too. Others find that their tongue swells or they get a pain in the chest and have difficulty breathing. It is really important for these people to get help as soon as this happens.

Reactions like this are called anaphylactic shock. They can be so bad that people may die. However, this hardly ever happens, especially to children, and there is a medicine called **adrenaline** that can be taken straightaway to make people better.

Why do insects sting?

Small insects like wasps and bees mostly use stings to protect themselves. They cannot kill the creatures that try to eat them, but their stings can hurt. Stinging insects are usually brightly coloured, often with red or yellow and black. This warns **predators** not to attack and lets them fly about in safety.

Most of us look forward to summer and lazy days in the sun, but stinging insects can be a nuisance for people with insect allergies.

Taking care in the sun

Whether or not you have an allergy to insect stings, it is no fun to be stung. It is hard to avoid insects in summer, but here is a list of things you can do that should help.

- Don't drink from cans. Stinging insects may crawl inside a can, attracted by the sugary drink and you won't spot them. The most dangerous place to be stung is in the mouth.

- Always wear shoes outside. Bees often sit on clover that grows in the grass and they will sting you if you tread on them.

If an insect lands on your food – don't panic! If you keep still and calm it will usually fly away after a few seconds without doing you any harm at all.

- When you go out in summer, wear cool tops with long sleeves, and trousers rather than shorts to keep your skin covered. This will also protect you from sunburn.

- Food attracts insects, so keep it covered up as much as you can if you are eating outside.

- Avoid wearing brightly coloured clothes, especially those made from flowery material, as these seem to attract bees and other insects.

Responding to insect allergies

In summer there are lots of insects about, most of which do not sting. Of the stinging insects, very few ever actually sting people. Even so, it does sometimes happen. What can allergy sufferers do if they get stung?

Once anyone has had an allergic reaction to an insect sting, they are likely to have a similar or worse reaction the next time. In case they do suffer a serious reaction, doctors give them a kit called the Epi-pen. It can stop any dangerous reactions.

Sting beater – the Epi-pen

The Epi-pen kit contains **adrenaline**, which is given by injection. People with sting allergies are trained to inject themselves with this medicine if they are ever unfortunate enough to be stung. Even children can be trained to use the Epi-pen themselves. It is easy and does not hurt a bit. It is vital that people with sting allergies inject themselves with the Epi-pen as soon as they are stung, so they have to keep it with them or nearby at all times.

Meet Ben

My name is Ben and I'm nearly ten years old. I'm allergic to insect stings so I've got to be really careful in summer. It's not like having an allergy to something like strawberries, where you can just choose not to eat them. It's really hard to avoid being stung by wasps and bees because stings can happen to anyone, just about anywhere. I like playing outside in summer, so I have some medicine to take in case I do get stung.

I've got a special injection pack with my medicine in. It's a special kind of injection that I just tap against my thigh – it's really easy to do. When I go to school I keep the kit in the fridge in the staff room. If I get stung, my friends and teachers know that I need to have an injection straightaway. I know I need to be careful, but my allergy doesn't stop me doing what I like in summer. I just have to remember to take my adrenaline kit with me wherever I go.

Glossary

adrenaline medicine that can make you better if you have a severe allergic reaction

allergen substance, that even in microscopic (very small) amounts, like pollen dust, causes an allergic reaction in some people

antibiotic medicine that can help or cure some kinds of infection

antibody substance made by the white cells of the immune system, that reacts to 'intruders' such as germs or allergens

antigen germ or natural substance that causes the body to produce antibodies

antihistamine medicine to treat allergic reactions. It works by stopping the effect of histamine.

asthma narrowing of the air passages that causes people to wheeze or cough. Asthma symptoms are often brought on by allergies.

contagious likely to pass on a rash or disease by touch or other contact. Allergy rashes are not contagious.

dander hairs and flakes of skin from animals, on which their saliva (spit) and other fluids collect

eczema skin condition that causes itching and a red rash. In some cases it can cause blisters and feel hot, too.

germs tiny living things that you can see only with a powerful microscope. Some germs can cause disease if they get into your body.

histamine chemical produced by the body that causes many allergic reactions

immune system parts of the body that work together to defend it from infection and fight disease

inhaler device which enables people with asthma to breathe in their medicines

inherit an inherited characteristic, e.g. blue eyes, is one that is passed from parents to their young

lancet small device with a sharp point used to prick the surface of the skin

lungs parts of the body used for breathing. Your lungs are inside your chest.

pollen tiny grains of plants (grasses, trees and flowers). Pollen can cause hay fever and asthma symptoms.

predator animal that kills and eats other animals

rhinitis condition that makes people sneeze, have a runny and blocked nose and itchy, watery eyes

skin prick test test used to find out what causes a person's allergy. Tiny amounts of possible allergens are put into the arm with a small lancet. If the area becomes swollen, the substance is a cause of the person's allergy.

symptom something that your body feels that tells you something is wrong and that you have a disease or illness

trigger something that brings on (triggers or sets off) an allergic reaction in a person

white blood cell type of cell found in the blood. White blood cells are part of the body's immune system. Some white blood cells, attack any germs that have entered the body.

Helpful books and addresses

BOOKS
Body Systems: Eating and Digestion, Angela Royston, Heinemann Library, 1996

The Human Machine: The Power Pack, Sarah Angliss, Belitha Press, 1999

When It's Hard to Breathe, Judith Condon, Franklin Watts, 1998

ORGANIZATIONS AND WEBSITES
Action Against Allergy provides support and information for people with allergies, as well as a newsletter for members.
(AAA) Action Against Allergy
PO Box 278
Twickenham, Middlesex
TW1 4QQ
Telephone: 020 8892 2711
E-mail: AAA@actionagainstallergy.freeserve.co.uk
Websites: www.actionagainstallergy.co.uk
www.merton-books.co.uk

The British Allergy Foundation (BAF)
Deepdene House
30 Bellgrove Road
Welling, Kent
DA16 3PY
Telephone: 020 8303 8525
Helpline: 020 8303 8583
Website: www.allergyfoundation.com

The Anaphylaxis Campaign
Anaphylaxis is a severe allergic reaction. This group provides help and support for families where someone has a severe food allergy.
PO Box 275
Farnborough
Hampshire GU14 6SX
Telephone: 01252 542029
Website: www.anaphylaxis.org.uk

IN AUSTRALIA
ASEHA (Allergy, Sensitivity and Environmental Health Association Qld Inc)
PO Box 96
Margate QLD 4019 Australia
Telephone/Fax: (07) 3284 8742
E-mail: asehaqld@powerup.com.au
Website: www.asehaqld.org.au

Index